# PERSUASION: A comprehensive guide on how to master the power of persuasion

# Table of Contents

# Introduction

Persuasion is a pervasive force in every facet of communication today. Unfortunately, the idea of persuasion has gotten a negative connotation over the years. It is often associated with manipulation, brainwashing or deceit. Adolph Hitler or Osama bin Laden are typical examples that are responsible for this negative view of persuasion. For this reason, people are reluctant to study or inform themselves about the power of persuasion.

The comparison of persuasion with a tool, which can be put to good or bad use, is important though. According to the ancient Greek philosopher, Aristotle, persuasion in the right hands can be used to work the greatest deeds, but when used wrongly, it can cause the worst harm.

This brings us to the intentions of the persuader – whether an influence attempt is ethically correct or not, depends mainly on the motives of the persuader, or what exactly the persuader is striving to reach. It depends only secondarily on the strategies he or she is employing.

Since persuasion is so pervasive, not informing ourselves about persuasion in every day circumstances is therefore completely naïve. Of course we can avoid learning about it, but we cannot avoid encountering it every day. Having the necessary knowledge about how to react in persuasive situations, as well as the integrity on how to ethically use one's knowledge about persuasion, would constitute the ideal therefore.

This book will offer an overview on how persuasion works, as well as why it works like it does. General advice will be given on how to improve persuasion skills, while staying within the correct ethical borders, as well as on how to be able to resist being persuaded and avoid influence attempts, especially when they are unethical.

# Benefits of Persuasion

Despite the negative connotation to persuasion, it is and can be used in positive ways as well. People who won the Nobel Peace Prize or the Pulitzer Prize have used persuasion as well. Most people who use persuasion successfully, have completely respectable careers. This could include for example diplomats, motivational speakers, recruiters, and many more.

A few positive changes persuasion has been and is able to make for the sake of the community, are for example:

- Peace agreements between two or more nations in times of war
- Fundraising for charity organizations
- Convincing of motorists to use their seatbelts
- Encouraging of drug-users to seek professional help
- Encouraging one's football-team as coach
- Urging of children not to get in a stranger's car, etc.

It is thus clear, that persuasion has a positive side as well, and is the cornerstone of many positive social aims and projects. Most of the positive things in everyday life and in the world in general was and is dependent on persuasion therefore.

When considering the importance of persuasion as a positive force in life as well, the studying of persuasion becomes much easier to motivate. Four main benefits of informing oneself, or studying the role of persuasion in human communication, are the instrumental function, the knowledge and awareness function, the defensive function and the debunking function.

- Instrumental function:
It is called the instrumental function, since persuasion is here used as an instrument to achieve something. Learning more about persuasion will thus help us to become better persuaders ourselves and achieve what we strive for.

When we take ethics into account, persuasion is an important basic element in communication. Being competent in communication means to act effectively and appropriately, as well as achieving our goals through ways that are fitting.

A successful persuader should know how to adapt his or her message to fit the frame of reference of the audience and the strategies of persuading should be thought over and planned as well. Cultural and social norms of the situation should be taken into consideration as well. The message should be arranged and organized in the best possible way.

- Knowledge and awareness function:
This advantage of studying persuasion refers to one's knowledge and awareness of the different types of persuasive processes. Knowledge about persuasive processes will immediately give one power over these situations.

Habitual persuasion, in the case of the persuader, will also be overcome with the gaining of more knowledge. People in business or marketing often get comfortable with certain techniques or ways of persuading. They should be able though to adapt strategies to different situations and audiences. Successful persuasion is marked to be different in all situations and circumstances.

- Defensive function:
The third advantage of understanding persuasion is to be able to defend oneself. One will be able to have better judgement when being persuaded. Many people also do not realize the effect persuasion has on them, through for example advertisements or marketing campaigns. Therefore being informed about these persuasive methods can only help.

- Debunking function:
The last advantage of informing ourselves about persuasion, is that it enables us to see and understand the real truth in persuasive situations, instead of easily being cheated and persuaded.

# How persuasion is used in present time

Persuasion techniques have their origin already in ancient times. The Greeks emphasized rhetoric and elocution as absolutely important characteristics for a successful politician. The Greek philosopher, Aristotle, reasoned that learning the art of persuasion is important to everyone though, and not only to politicians. . Aspects that Aristotle believed could be relevant to everyday life at that time, were for example the importance of persuasion as teaching tool and the fact that it was the only way to defend oneself in certain situations.

Today, when we start to pay attention, we realize that the number of persuasive messages around us in our everyday lives, are basically uncountable. Persuasion is therefore pervasive. Everywhere, we are exposed to influence attempts – explicit and implicit. (To add to this number, there are just as many 'potentially' persuasive messages, since whether a fact or a situation is persuasive or not, can just as well be in the eye of the beholder.) According to various statistics, the average person is exposed to three hundred to three thousand persuasive messages per day.

We might think that we are not easily persuaded by outside influences, that we have the ability to see the truth in situations and that we are able to come up with our own conclusions. The fact is that we are not always aware of all the subtle persuasions of everyday life. Persuasion is therefore not restricted only to determined salesmen or special sales at the local supermarket. It is thus clear that persuasion is a central feature of human communication in present time.

Persuasion today occurs in many different ways:

-       Regarding marketing, the first is through word of mouth. This might sound a bit old-fashioned, but it is true. The average consumer has become cynical. General trust among the public in advertisements is disappearing. Consumers start to trust advice from their friends instead. Therefore, about ninety percent of recommendations happens offline. The reason why interpersonal influence is becoming more important again, is because it appears for the consumer to be more genuine.

-       For this reason, social networks are becoming powerful too, seen from a marketing point of view. Using social networks for marketing purposes, is called 'buzz' marketing and is dependent on friendships to function. It has several advantages for the marketer, especially since it is much cheaper than traditional marketing techniques.
New media, like Facebook or Twitter, are therefore not only entertaining mediums anymore. They are becoming important mediums for influence as well. The presence of social influence is very clear here. Companies are even able to track and monitor social media by using software which is able to determine the public's general 'mood' or opinions about a certain product. This software picks up all words related to feelings or opinions, and thus determines the general opinion of the public. Social media influence politics as well, in the same way as with marketing.

-       'Gamification' is only another way of persuasion becoming part of everyday life. It creates interest among the consumers, as well as involvement. This refers to downloadable applications for cell phones. Through these applications the consumer can earn points or badges, and many other 'rewards'. The consumers are therefore motivated and come back for more. An example could be the promotion of health insurance, where the consumers are encouraged to do all kinds of fitness tests to earn points, or to buy certain healthy products for other rewards, etc. This is very successful, since people enjoy the challenge of competition and games.

Other examples are applications to encourage education, or to make people aware of certain social causes.

There is critique against this kind of persuasion though – instead of learning for the sake of becoming more intelligent and successful in life, as well as due to the motivation of being able to study and understand the writings of ancient masters, the main motivation for learning in 'gamification' is to earn more points, or to win some reward.

-        Persuasion still occurs in the science today. Scientists have to convince other scientists and the public of their research findings, that their research has merit scientifically and socially. It is said that a successful scientist does not only need the necessary scientific knowledge, but also needs to be able to defend his or her theory successfully, especially when funds are needed.

-        Persuasion also occurs in the arts. Many pieces of art are not only created for aesthetic purposes. Artists in general have strong opinions. These opinions, whether political or social, are then expressed through their art. Therefore, instead of using words, comments on social conditions or society are made.

- Alcoholics Anonymous is also an example of where persuasion plays an important role. Through persuasion and encouragement, these people are helped. This applies to all other forms of group support, for example weight-loss, drug abuse, etc.

- Persuasion in the military is very important. An example of where effective persuasion techniques were used on innocent people, was in the Korean War with America. Large numbers of captured American soldiers willingly cooperated with the enemy. It was thought that they were tortured or beaten to act like this, but they were simply brainwashed by having to answer questions about American politics, for example freedom, equality or democracy. The brainwashing through persuasion went on till the soldiers started to believe the point of view of the enemy. For this reason, the military in general pays a lot of attention as well on education in politics as well.

An early Chinese philosopher of war, Sun Tzu, wrote a book on the significance of persuasion in the military. He emphasized that the use of the correct strategy and psychology can help prevent war in general and the loss of many lives. He said that to win many battles are less of a skill than to subdue the enemy without any fighting.

- Bumper stickers are a simple example of persuasion as well.

- The computerized gadgets in new cars telling the driver how much gasoline is used, therefore encouraging him or her to drive in a different way to save more gasoline is a form of persuasion as well.

- The X-Box or Play Station games that encourage players for example to be physically involved, is also persuasion.

Ways in which persuasion differs in present time, and reasons why:

1.      Like already mentioned, persuasion is pervasive, meaning that the number of messages in present times are of course considerably more than in ancient times - the main reason being that persuasive messages are able to be transferred or travel much easier and faster than in early times.

2.      Persuasion has become an important industry nowadays. There are huge companies whose existence depends solely on persuasion (e.g. marketing or advertisements companies, etc.) as well as other businesses that are dependent on persuasion for selling their products or services.

3.      Persuasion in present times are much more subtle – of course there are many obvious commercials or marketing projects, but persuasion has become an art in dealing with each other every day…

4.      Persuasion has become much more complex, due to consumers being more diverse. The message and medium of persuasion are therefore only a small part of many factors to be taken into consideration during the persuasion process.

# The seven drivers of human motivation

Motivation is the reason behind us taking action – the driving force behind it all. It initiates and sustains a goal-orientated vision and action in life. The kind of driving force behind each action is different in each situation. These driving forces could be biological, social, emotional or personal.

In 1943, Maslow said that people are motivated to fulfil certain needs. When the first is fulfilled, the person will start to strive to fulfil the next one. He therefore invented a certain hierarchy of needs. One should first fulfil the more basic levels of needs, before trying to fulfil the higher levels of needs – the lower levels of needs being the most basic needs, for example food, water, etc. and the highest level of need being self-actualization.

Unfortunately, life experiences often slow down or stops growth and progress as a person. Therefore only seldom do people reach the top level of self-actualization.

It is possible to add one more step to this hierarchy, namely the transcendence stage. This is only possible after self-actualization and means to help other people to achieve self-actualization.

## Biological and Physiological needs

These are the most basic needs in order to survive. They include food, water, air, sleep, a 'shelter' or place to live in, sex, warmth, etc.

Satisfying sexual urges therefore falls in this category. Males, as well as females, will do everything possible to attract the right partner. In present time, this is the main driving force behind for example, the industry of cosmetics. People buy the products in order to be more attractive for the opposite gender.

# Safety needs

After having fulfilled the physiological needs, self-protection is the next. The concept of safety needs in present times are of course different than it was in the early times of human history. These needs today include for example a relatively safe neighbourhood, the possibility to have access to health care, a steady income, employment, order, law, etc.

# Love and belongingness needs

After having fulfilled the physiological and safety-needs, one needs affection, one needs to feel loved, one needs to feel that one belongs somewhere. This includes intimacy as well.

Humans are social beings, and therefore need relationships, for example family relationships, normal friendships, romantic relationships, etc. It is through these relationships that one gets a feeling of belonging somewhere. The need to be accepted somewhere is therefore a strong driving force as well.

# Esteem needs

These include self-esteem, achievement or mastery in general, independence, status, etc. The reason why this is an important driving force behind people's actions, is because people need to feel valued and respected in some way in society. Self-esteem needs include for example social recognition and worth as a person.

Contrary to this, an unhealthy or low self-esteem and inferior feelings can prevent someone to do what they strive for – therefore actually a form of negative motivation or persuasion. Just being accepted by other people will not fulfil these needs, till one is able to accept oneself internally first.

# Cognitive needs
These include knowledge, meaning, etc. One cannot go through life uninformed about everything, or with no education.

# Aesthetic needs
Search and appreciation for aesthetic elements in life.

# Self-Actualization needs
Self-actualizing needs include the search for personal growth. Self-actualization means being able to do or become what one desires. This can be a successful businessman, an excellent musician or athlete. Without having fulfilled this need, one will always be frustrated and feel unfulfilled. Therefore it is important to realize one's personal potential.

# The need for attachment

Since the day we were born, we have a biological need in life for attachment, meaning to be in a relationship. It is therefore a biological 'must' to have this fulfilled. We are who we are, and reach in life everything within a complicated network of relationships. Emotional attachment is the driving force behind our existence, growing, changing as a person and reaching things in life in general. It is not possible to avoid attachment or relationships, since our lives are 'populated' with other people who are all part of complicated relationship networks.

Developing these relationships, is fundamental in our growth as a person. We therefore need a person or persons who are attuned to our attachment-needs, and who is able to fulfil these needs.

People do not outgrow these needs for relationships. It is exactly this need that makes us human. Even when we are adults already, we still (most often subconsciously) attach ourselves to people we believe will be able to satisfy these needs. When finally our needs in this regard are met, we can develop as a person, be creative and expansive for example, as well as intimate.

Unfortunately, old, unmet relationship- or attachment-needs can in certain circumstances influence our present day relationships and needs. A feeling of insecurity and emotional disturbance develop when a person's attachment-needs are repeatedly not met. The person then automatically adapts to this by developing an attachment style or pattern compensating for the unfulfilled needs in the relationship(s).

Relationship-needs in more detail include the following:
- Security need
- Within a relationship: affirmation and significance
- Acceptance by the other person in the relationship
- The other person in the relationship should be stable and dependable
- Confirmation regarding personal experience
- Self-definition
- Making a difference in the other person's life
- The other person in the relationship should be able to offer initiative and love

# Personal desires

Personal desires are goals that are important for the individual, in contrast to desires of a family, a community, etc.

It is important for us to achieve our personal goals or to fulfil our personal desires. This helps us to develop into well-balanced, healthy (physically and mentally) people. We will feel more positive about ourselves, as a person as well as professionally, when we succeed in setting and fulfilling our personal goals. We will feel more productive, could earn a better income, all contributing to a better and higher self-esteem. Important though, is that until we are able to fulfil our personal desires and goal, we will not be in a position to help other people in their pursuit of happiness and fulfilment. For this reason, the fulfilment of personal desires are much more important and less egoistic than we think.

# Social needs

Social needs are crucial to all people, even when some people would not like to admit it. According to Maslow's hierarchy (mentioned earlier), social needs include for example family, friendships, romantic relationships, churches, and other community groups. In Maslow's pyramid, social needs follow the most basic needs, and are more important than for example self-esteem or self-actualization. Social needs are necessary to develop and grow as a person. Loneliness, depression and anxiety are the results of not feeling loved or appreciated somewhere.

# Emotional requirements

There are five categories when it comes to core emotional needs. When these are met, a person will be content, and be able to be concerned about other people's well-being as well.

Core emotional needs:

- Every person needs to feel safe, nurtured, stable and accepted.
- Everyone needs to feel competent with a sense of identity.
- One needs to feel free in expressing his or her own emotions and needs.
- One should be able or allowed to simply be spontaneous.
- One has to live in a world with realistic limits.

# What people avoid

Certain toxic behaviour patterns result in pushing people away from each other. These toxic behaviours damage relationships, growth personally and professionally, health of the person, as well as everyone around him or her. Although nobody is perfect, some people are more balanced and aware, not to act in such a way regularly. In case it happens frequently, one might consider outside help to solve the problem.

- Being envious:
Envy happens when someone does not count his or her own blessings, but only the blessings of someone else or other people. Such a person should remember that it is *his* or *her* journey through life, and that it has nothing to do with other people. Life is not a competition with other people. It could be seen as a competition with oneself though – in a positive way – by comparing oneself with what kind of person one was yesterday, and what kind of person one is today.

- Taking things personally:
It is difficult to live and get along with people who believe everything happening to them is meant to harm or humiliate them. It is important to remember that what people do and say to someone, rather reflects on who *they* are, rather than on the person they are talking to or doing something to. The way people reacts to someone is all about their own wounds, experiences and perspectives. Too much sadness and disappointment in people's lives are due to them taking things too personally. Therefore, someone should rather let go of others' opinions and follow their own wisdom and intuition.

- Acting like a victim:
When someone believes he or she is a victim and has no power over life, it keeps that person stuck. People sometimes underestimate the power or influence they can have over their own lives. They simply have to believe in themselves and in reality.

- Let go of pain or loss:

  Change is always difficult, therefore letting go of pain, love, guilt, or loss, will not be easy. Letting go of something or an emotion, could be in some cases the healthier path forward though. It is thus important that someone frees him- or herself emotionally from the past.

- Negative thinking:

  Some people tend to think only about the negative part of life, for example all the terrible things that did happen, are happening or can happen, the unfairness of life, etc. This is not just normal pessimism, but a permanent negative mind-set. Living as if everything is against one, is a view of life that can be and should be changed.

- Lack of self-control:

  Not being able to manage one's emotions, makes it difficult for the people around that person. This include for example screaming at the grocer, or bursting out in tears in public places, etc. When someone finds him- or herself in such a condition, it might be a solution to find outside help. A change of perspective(s) on life in general might be beneficial.

- Superficial judging of other people:

  It is better not to judge other people so easily, since it is seldom possible to know and understand their circumstances completely. It will be better to simply let them be, and to continuo with one's own journey through life.

- Lack of empathy:

There exists no reason or motivation allowing or justifying people to be cruel to each other.

In the media, cases are reported every day where people kill, hurt, or backstab each other. Even online, people write hurtful remarks, using their anonymity.

- Cheating because you can:

Integrity is the solution to be successful. One should not cheat someone simply because one knows one will get away with it. The person who is the fool in the end is definitely the cheater, and not the cheated person. This includes being morally correct in all circumstances.

- Hiding your true identity

It is difficult for people to connect to someone, if that person is not comfortable with who he or she is. Being able to just be oneself, is absolutely necessary, no matter one's age, sex, race, religion, etc. Everyone is unique in a way, and nobody needs to be self-conscious or shy because of this. If one does not feel comfortable in certain circumstances or work environment, one should not change oneself as a person – it is better to stay oneself and change circumstances or one's work environment then.

- Need for constant approval:

People who are dependent on constant approval by the people around them, are as well exhausting and difficult to live with. Life is about more than what someone achieves (or not) in the eyes of colleagues or friends. One should therefore keep the bigger picture in mind. Life is about one's journey, what one learns one the way, how and whom one helps, and growing as a person oneself.

- Being perfectionistic:

One should keep in mind that being a perfectionist in this world, will only result in frustration and disappointment. One needs an open mind, to allow the imperfect house to become a comfortable, happy-filled house, the imperfect partner to become understanding and dependable and the imperfect job to become a successful career.

# Persuasion techniques

Much has been written about persuasion techniques, since it has become quite a specialized part of communication today.

When studying persuasion, it will help to go back to Maslow's hierarchy of human needs. Although there are many theories and steps to follow when trying to persuade someone, persuasion will only be effective if one's 'aim' of persuasion fits in the pyramid of human needs from Maslow. For example, it should help the person in some way to attain self-actualization, or it should somehow help fulfil the necessary social needs.

Important is that one should adapt one's persuasion techniques according to the person or audience to be persuaded. To be taken into consideration, are for example interest, experiences, beliefs, attitudes, motivations, thoughts, values, personality, etc. The same persuasion techniques will not be successful under all circumstances.

Also, one should be completely convinced oneself, before trying to convince another person or audience. One has to be mentally prepared and ready to persuade.

There are three D's to remember:

- Discover: one has to discover what exactly the other person or audience needs to hear.

- Design: one has to design a persuasive argument.

- Deliver: one has to deliver the argument with passion and purpose.

It is possible to construct a Checklist for Persuasion:

# Beliefs and Values

In order to know which approach to take, it will help to know and understand the beliefs and values of one's audience.

Beliefs refer to those things that people simply accept as the truth, whether it is proven or not. Beliefs typically come from for example experience, culture, environment, etc. People then tend to believe the same things as the people around them, and act accordingly.

Values are less superficial than beliefs, since people commit more consciously to these. Values are more seriously contemplated. To change a value is much harder than changing a belief.

# Change

One must be able to motivate one's audience to change/to be persuaded. It is normal for people to always choose the most comfortable solution, to choose the solution which does not need them to leave their comfort zone. People prefer the solution which will result in the least resistance. Unfortunately change is the only way to 'lift' us out of our daily patterns in which we are stuck.

One should determine how resistant one's audience is to change in general. It will help to be prepared to approach the matter from the right angle.

Change in people's lives can happen in three different ways:

- Drastic change: One is forced to change due to life-threatening events (for example a heart attack), personal tragedy or the loss of one's job.

- Gradual change: When someone changes over time, due to for example personal relationships or normal events in life.
- Internal change: When someone consciously decides to change, whether due to inspiration or desperation.

With change, three things have to be kept in mind:

- There has to exist enthusiasm to commit to a long term change.
- The person or audience has to be willing to sacrifice what is necessary for the change, for example continuing even when tired, etc.
- It must be clear what the end result of the change will be.

Obstacles that prevent change most often, are lack of knowledge and motivation, as well as fear. One should therefore be able to 'paint a picture' for one's audience about how the future will look like for them after the change.

# Acceptance

Before trying to persuade someone or an audience, the persuader has to know what the current acceptance level of the person or audience is. It is possible to determine this by asking a few short questions to oneself:

- What does the person or audience already know about the 'persuasion topic'?

- Is the person or audience interested in this topic?

- What is the background of the person or audience?

- Is there already some support in favour of the topic?

- What are the beliefs of the person or audience?

One should never take persuasion too far though. Some people are not able to read the other person or people well enough, to know when to stop. If persuasion or power is used wrongly, the person will lose trust and it will not be possible to ever persuade them again. A sixth sense is necessary in order to understand and feel when enough is enough in the persuasion process.

# Listening

We often think that we are good listeners, while in reality we are not. It is important to be a good listener if we intend to persuade someone or an audience. Following are five mistakes we often make:

-       Often, instead of listening, we are only thinking of what to say next in the conversation. We are therefore basically planning our own talking, without listening and reacting on what the other person or people have to say.

-       We are not always concentrating, thinking of other things while the person is talking.

-       Often, we jump to conclusions, instead of waiting for the other person to finish talking. We think we know what the person wants to say, and put words into his/her mouth.

-       When someone is not able to deliver a good 'speech' from his/her side, or when this person does not look or come across as attractive, we often judge this person without listening carefully what they are saying.

-       It takes much more mental effort and involvement to be a good listener, than most people think.

Advice on how to be a good listener:

- Allow the other person to speak, while giving him or her undivided attention. One should not allow one's surroundings to distract one.
- Look directly at the person while he or she is talking. Leaning forward a little will indicate that one is interested and concerned.
- One should show interest in the person while he or she is talking. One does not have to talk oneself necessarily, but nodding one's head will show that one is interested.
- Ask questions from the person to keep the conversation going, instead of talking oneself.
- Encourage the person to talk more by using silence. Gaining more information will also help one to know better how to go ahead with the persuasion process.
- Wait a moment before replying or continuing with the conversation. This will show the other person that one is really thinking about what they were saying.

Listening is very important, especially since one has to adapt one's persuasion process throughout to the other person – listening will help one to adapt it correctly.

# Personality types

When one understands the different types of personalities, we will know better how to go ahead persuading someone or an audience. Of course nobody is hundred percent predictable, but it is possible to categorize people broadly into a few categories.

Each personality type will of course determine how one will approach one's persuasion. These types include people who are logical, emotional, extroverts, introverts, desperate, inspired, assertive, amiable, etc.

Someone who has a lot of experience and is able to distinguish different personality types from each other, will be able to adapt his/her argument immediately to accommodate the other person and to persuade him/her more convincingly.

# Structuring one's argument

For a message to be persuasive, it has to consist of at least two basic elements. This include is the substance (facts, information) and the form (order of information, pattern). This is what makes an argument understandable. If an argument is not clear, the automatic response one will get from the other person or audience, is 'no'.

One should also remember that one needs to focus on one issue only, and not ten different ones, since this can cause confusion as well.

Also, one should be careful not to offend the other person or audience on sensitive issues during the persuasion process.

When structuring one's argument, one should pay attention to the following:

- One has to create an interest among the audience about one's topic – there has to be a reason for listening. It should immediately be clear what is in it for each one of them. One should manage to get the attention of the audience right at the beginning, by giving a good reason for them to listen. Only then is there any hope in bringing across one's message.

- One should clearly state the problem in the beginning. Try to think of ways this could possibly affect the other person or the people from the audience. Thus, one makes them aware of a problem they have and one suggests to them then how it could be solved.

- Evidence makes one's argument easier to believe. It makes it possible for the audience to not only rely on oneself, but also on statistics, testimonies, examples, etc.

- Next, one should mention the solution. One already created the possible need among the audience by stating the problem, therefore one should suggest the solution. One should explain how this solution can help them in general, as well as in achieving their goals.

- Finally, one should make it clear to the person or audience what is expected from them, or where and how they become involved. The 'call to action' is the most important part of the whole persuasion process. One should build the whole argument around the ending part. The 'call to action' part should be easy and simple for everyone to understand and follow.

One should include the following in one's argument as well:

- Repetition: Repetition is important for effective persuasion. It leads to familiarity to one's ideas, which results in positive associations. It improves comprehension in general. One should make sure that one's audience understands and knows exactly what one is talking about, as well as what they are supposed to do.

- Theme: Themes are remembered easily, and will contribute to one's argument coming across as more flowing and better organized. Themes make it possible for people to more easily remember the core of one's message, as well as understand it.
- Simplicity and brevity: One should rather keep one's message as simple and short as possible. It will be clearer and more easily remembered. Opt for simple terms all the way through, and make points clear and direct.
- Timing: In an argument, it is important to make use of good timing regarding one's arguments. The first and last parts of an argument will be remembered the best, therefore the opening and end parts are powerful tools.

- Choices: Regarding drawing conclusions, one phenomenon has to be kept in mind. If a person tells another exactly what to do, there is most often an automatic negative reaction to this, namely to reject it. People need to feel free and they need to feel that if they do something, that it was their own choice. In a persuasion situation therefore, one should offer two or three structured choices (all of the choices satisfying the persuader's needs). Only then, the person or audience will be easier persuaded and not feel pressured.
- Inoculation: With inoculation is meant to prepare one's audience to possible opposing viewpoints, almost like a flu shot – by mentioning the opposing viewpoints in one's argument, one increases one's credibility, as well as one's ability to persuade.

An example is 'preparing' teenagers against smoking, using drugs, or pregnancy. By telling them in advance the possible arguments people with bad influence might use, will help them to be better prepared when they are confronted in real life.

The seeds for perfect persuasion are being prepared mentally to persuade, knowing one's audience, as well as the structuring of one's argument.

More general techniques include the following:

1. Due to timing and circumstances, not all people are persuadable at a given time or place. Therefore, rather focus on those that are persuadable.

2. One has to learn how to talk to people about themselves, because someone's own life and responsibilities are the only things that will interest them. Only through interest one can persuade.

3. When someone persist in asking/persuading over a long time, while demonstrating value, it will pay off eventually.

4. Paying sincere compliments to people will help in creating a positive feeling towards one.

5. Create scarcity – for example a sale that ends in a few days, or a one-time special offer in buying a product, etc. The limited availability creates the impression that the product is very popular.

6. One needs to transfer energy to one's audience or the other person, instead of draining them. The most successful 'persuaders' have this characteristic.

7. Be calm, unemotional and detached in moments of conflict. This will give one more power.

8. One could imitate the body language (within limits) of the person one wants to persuade. This will create a sense of empathy.

9. One can use reciprocation, meaning to create an obligation by doing something nice for someone else.

10. One should be confident in one's speech – people are easier persuaded by someone who is confident.

11. One can start the conversation with 'yes'- questions. This makes it easier to finally get a 'yes'-answer for the selling of the product.

# Resistant factors

There exist two kinds of persuasion, which influences also the level of resistance against later persuasion attempts with different points of view.

The first kind, is the central or systematic route to persuasion. This is when the person or audience pays careful attention to the message, thinking carefully about the relevant information and logic behind it all. People approach persuasive situations like this, when they feel that the message is relevant to them, when they have experience or knowledge in this area, or when they feel in a way responsible in this area of influence. With this kind of persuasion, the content of the message needs to be of high quality, rather than well-presented with empty words.

The second kind of persuasion is the peripheral or heuristic kind of persuasion. In this case, the person or audience will rather pay attention to other superficial aspects of the message in general. This happens when the person to be persuaded is not much motivated, has little time or ability to try to understand and think over the real or deeper meaning of the message. Attention is rather paid to 'source' characteristics and 'message' characteristics. Source characteristics refers to aspects, such as whether the persuader is attractive, or whether the persuader appears to be credible. Message characteristics refers to the number of arguments for example, or whether the conclusion was clear, or not.

When someone who was originally persuaded through systematic persuasion happens to end up in a persuasion attempt by the opposite point of view, he or she will less likely change his or her mind, since during the persuasion process, all relevant evidence and all logic behind it all was thoroughly thought over.

When a person who was originally persuaded through peripheral persuasion ends up in a second persuasion attempt by the opposite point of view, the chances are much bigger for this person to change his or her mind again.

# Reactance:

When somebody persists too much in trying to persuade someone, this person might become annoyed and resentful. He or she can even take on the point of view completely opposite to that of the persuader, due to feeling forced to do something he or she does not want to do. This is called the process of reactance. The reason for this is that the person being persuaded feels that it is a direct threat to his or her personal freedom. Everyone likes to and needs to feel free and independent. This can also be called 'negative attitude change', meaning that after the process of persuasion, the person being persuaded feels even stronger about his or her point of view against that of the persuader. It therefore could have a boomerang effect.

# Forewarning or prior knowledge:

Research has shown that when someone is forewarned about a possible persuasion situation, the person will not be so easily persuaded. The knowledge of such a persuasion situation beforehand, activates certain cognitive processes which make being persuaded more difficult.

It also makes it possible for the person to find counterarguments, as well as informing him- or herself better about the persuasive message.

# Counter-arguing:

By arguing against a persuasion attempt, someone can actively resist being persuaded. By doing so, it helps the person being persuaded to develop a general 'self-defense' against persuasion.

# Attitude inoculation:

Like mentioned earlier, research has proven that by exposing a person to weak counter-arguments before trying to persuade him or her, will prevent the person from changing his or her mind later, after having been exposed to all the counter-arguments as well. It works in the same way as immunization does in the process of fighting serious illnesses. The person has the time and possibility to develop a kind of 'defense' against the stronger influence and are therefore less likely to be persuaded.

Therefore, inoculation allows a person to develop his or her own arguments against the persuasion topic, and thus become more resistant against being persuaded.

# Avoidance:

By ignoring or simply filtering out facts and information that do not agree with one's pre-existing beliefs or values, is another way of resisting persuasion. This process is called 'selective avoidance'. One therefore accepts or listens only to information that is consistent with one's own point of view. It is a fact that people pay more attention to for example someone talking, when this person's point of view is consistent with their own way of thinking.

# Attitude polarization:

This happens when people interpret mixed information and eventually end up with a stronger point of view consistent with their values and beliefs, than they had before the persuasion.

# Biased assimilation

By this kind of assimilation, the person evaluates counter-arguments as unreliable, and arguments consistent with their point of view as reliable.

# Questioning of the source

Through questioning the source of the counter-argument, the person is able to resist the persuasion.

# When persuasion techniques won't work

In some cases, even when the most professional persuasion techniques are used, trying to persuade someone or a group of people, will not work. The abovementioned aspects all applies here: cases of reactance (only one option to choose from, as well as too much persistence in the persuasion process), prior knowledge of a persuasion attempt, counter-arguing which re-inforces original values or points of view, inoculation, avoidance (when filtering out inconsistent information regarding one's original values or beliefs), attitude polarization (mixed feelings that re-inforce original values), biased assimilation (accepting only consistent arguments) and questioning of the source.

Like mentioned earlier, successful persuasion is also dependent on correct timing, circumstances and place. Regarding timing, people keep changing throughout their lives. Therefore successful persuasion depends on which moment in their lives they are confronted with the persuasion. Regarding circumstances, all the above mentioned factors fall into this category. Circumstances therefore include the kind of persuasion being used, whether the person is prepared for the persuasion or not, etc. Regarding place and/or background of the person being persuaded, aspects such as local beliefs, religion, family history, etc. will be determining factors.

# Conclusion

Persuasion is therefore an important component of communication nowadays and it does not necessarily need to have a negative connotation. Like mentioned already, persuasion has several benefits – when in the right hands and when used correctly. Few people realize how many things around them in every day life is the result of persuasion used in a positive way: all charity organizations, all group support institutions (like mentioned before), all 'green' organizations, etc.

Persuasion in present times differs a lot from ancient times of course, especially since it can be much more subtle today. Persuasion in the ancient times was mostly used in politics, and of course in doing business. For this reason, it is necessary to pay attention today if persuasion is used ethically correct or not.

As persuader, one needs to take into account the seven drivers of human motivation, as set apart in the hierarchy of human needs by Maslow. Only when the topic of persuading fits into this pyramid of needs, will the persuasion process be successful. Life is too fast and competitive for people today, to spend time and energy in persuaders with only selfish goals.

Other aspects to keep in mind as persuader, is every person's basic need for attachment or relationships. Within this network of relationships are aspects such as personal desires, social needs, emotional needs and what people avoid, that should be taken into consideration as well with the persuasion process. When the persuader is not well enough informed about these aspects, his or her chances are small to succeed in persuading. The importance of one's ability to relate to the person or audience being persuaded, is often overlooked.

Regarding persuasion techniques, one should first of all be able to decide which approach would be most successful with the specific person or audience. The rest of the necessary techniques will automatically fall into place. In some cases, the techniques necessary to persuade will need to be more informal, whereas in other scenarios the situation might require a formal approach only. The persuader will need to be able to distinguish between these necessities.

Resistant factors should be kept in mind by the persuader, as far as it is in his or her hands. When the persuader is aware of possible resistance factors, it will help him or her to adapt the approach of persuasion as is necessary. When someone or a group of people are not ready to be persuaded, it is important to know when to stop, and rather spend energy on those that are persuadable.

Concluding, one has to keep the ethical part in mind with the persuasion process. There exist the obvious ways of persuading, and then the more subtle ways of persuading that advertisers or people sometimes use to influence people subconsciously. This is done 'below' the conscious perception level of the public or person being persuaded. For this reason, this kind of persuasion (in advertisements for example) is illegal in the UK and Australia.

In general though, persuasion can serve a good purpose, as long as the intentions and end goal of the persuader is morally correct.

Persuasion is therefore a relevant and important issue nowadays about which people should inform themselves – an important part of human communication which can make life much easier.